AGNOSIS AND PAROUSIA

Other Works by Sandy Krolick

Вероника: Сибирская Сказка (Novel)
Veronika: The Siberian's Tale (Novel)
The Recovery of Ecstasy: Notebooks from Siberia
Apocalypse of Barbarians: Inquisitions on Empire
Conversations On A Country Path
Gandhi in the Postmodern Age
Recollective Resolve
Ethical Decision-making Styles
Культурныи критицизм
Myth, Mystery and Magic: Religion in Ancient Egypt
Russian Soul and Collapse of the West
Shambhala (Novel)
Misha (Novel)
On Being and Being Good
Q: Interpreting QAnon
A New Heaven and a New Earth
Philosophic Play
Babel Unhinged
The Siberian Shaman and Western Myth
Notebooks: Philosophical Memoirs

AGNOSIS AND PAROUSIA

SANDY KROLICK, PH.D.

ISLANDS PRESS
NEW YORK : ALTAI KRAI : FLORIDA

ISBN: 978-1-7350698-8-3

Cover art courtesy of:
Yuri Ivanov
Altai Krai, Russia

To live is to suffer;
to survive is to find some meaning in the suffering

Friederich Nietzsche

'Parousia' and Politics in America

1. Preface

Our current reflections lie just this side of a rather daunting crossroads in the history and philosophy of religion. Such placement should enable us to explore both cultural and existential dimensions of a relatively novel, and rather unsettling, instantiation of Christian faith today.

Religion in America has been increasingly used as a cudgel among surging numbers of apparently professed Christian faithful. This is so in spite of the fact that formal religious affiliation has waned among our populace over the past few decades. According to recent polling by the Pew Research group, approximately 63% of adults in the United States identified as Christian in the year 2021. That number was down from 75% in 2015 and 85% as recently as 1990. But diminishing institutional affiliation does not adequately reflect concrete reality on the ground, nor the weightiness of our current concerns. In fact, the challenge confronting us is not religious belief *per se*, but a uniquely contentious, hyper-conservative Christian plurality. This is especially the case in light of the clearly extreme views and apparent trajectory of a vociferous Christian Nationalism and its support among White Conservative Evangelicals.

We wish to unpack this religiously infused political situation, including its theological and philosophical underbelly, as well as its apparent apocalyptic interpretation of events currently unfolding. By means of a hermeneutic approach, we shall excavate the roots of an exploding political crisis here in the homeland, a crisis fueled by extremist mythologies guiding a rather novel incarnation of Christian faith today. In this respect, it will be necessary to understand the lifeworld animating an increasingly agitated segment of American conservatives. We must demonstrate how their passion is focussed on resuscitating a profoundly mythologized past and their desire for a dystopian return to some lost but glorious beginning — the presumed perfection of our national origins. In short, it is frightful to imagine that the potential re-election of an indicted former president may be heralded as a genuine *parousia* — the Second Coming of their savior — a situation we should anticipate with both fear and trembling.

2. Resolutely Apocalyptic

> *If we change our eschatology, we
> will change the world — and take
> dominion of it for the glory of God.*
> (1)

With statements like this, a growing cadre
of Christian Nationalists have expressed
their desire for the end of the world as we
know it. And while the nature of that *End
Time* is not clearly fleshed-out, we
understand that such believers intend for
the return of their political hero — the
'Orange Jesus' — to office of the President
of the United States. Before exploring the
concrete intention of such an apocalyptic
eschatology, we must first consider its real
foundation — its historical and apparently
biblical framework.

Obviously, we understand that this is not
the first or only proclamation of the
eschaton among the Christian faithful.
Even prior to the apocalyptic visions of St.
John in his *Revelation*, the Apostle Paul
was already proselytizing with thoroughly

eschatological language. Encouraging his followers at the church in Corinth, Paul wrote about the highly anticipated return of their Lord.

> *I give thanks to my God always for you because of the grace of God that has been given to you . . . so that you are not lacking in any spiritual gift as you wait for the revealing of our Lord Jesus Christ.* (2)

Of course, it was on his way to Damascus, in the midst of persecuting adherents of the new faith, that Paul (*née* Saul) underwent his own self-transforming experience of conversion. In *Acts of the Apostles*, we read:

> *Now as he was going along approaching Damascus, suddenly a light from heaven flashed around him. He fell to the ground and heard a voice saying to him, "Saul, Saul, why do you persecute me?"* (3)

This singular event became the foundation of Paul's *metanoia*, his spiritual awakening and conversion to the faith of those he had previously tormented. From that moment onwards, instead of persecuting believers, Paul became their most vocal advocate and defender — a missionary bent on spreading God's word. Look, for example, at Paul's brief reflection regarding his own conversion experience:

Last of all, as to one untimely born, he [Christ] appeared also to me. For I am the least of the apostles, unfit to be called an apostle, because I persecuted the church of God. But, by the grace of God I am what I am and his grace toward me has not been in vain. (4)

Although Paul's conversion is among the most notable in Christian history, this *metanoia* or 'change of heart' is not unlike other events of illumination in the history of religion, Christian or otherwise.

In his work on *The Phenomenology of Religious Life*, Martin Heidegger contends that the basic occurrence underlying any religious conversion is a mystical experience, an event or episode of ecstatic communion with the divine. Of course, such an episode lies at the very heart of Paul's spiritual rebirth. And from that moment onwards his preaching is firmly focussed on the *parousia* — the Second Coming of Jesus, and his salvific return to earth. As Paul notes in Thessalonians:

> *For since we believe that Jesus died and rose again, even so, through Jesus, God will bring with him those who have died.* (5)

While Christian Nationalists and Evangelicals alike anxiously await this world-transforming event, we are forced to reflect on the depth of the political challenge it poses for us today. The political posture of these movements appears poised to eclipse democratic rule in the hope of bearing witness to the unfolding of their sacred narrative, the dawning of 'a new heaven and a new earth' ruled over by a divinely sanctioned figure. And this now becomes the principal source of our greatest fear and concern — the potential for political upheaval grounded in a mythic-religious zeal for the *End Time*. For these faithful, it appears that our disgraced former President now represents a fresh incarnation of believers' salvific hope. As one political columnist characterized the situation earlier this year:

> *Trump's record aside, there is a more disturbing phenomenon going on among conservative Evangelicals: a Christian nationalist movement in which Trump can only be described as an irreplaceable figure whose political success is crucial to God's plan for redeeming a sinful world.* (6)

References to the former President's apparent status, and his divinely sanctioned mission, are now strewn throughout diverse press releases, news reports, articles, and, most especially, internet chatrooms. Just browse a sampling of those words supporting the former President. A brief post on *Gab* from early April (Easter) referencing Trump's trial, for example, reads: "*Seems there was someone else who was tortured and crucified this week.*"

Meanwhile, a shorter post on *Telegram* is even more bluntly apocalyptical. It reads: "*Good vs Evil. Biblical Times. Divine Timing.*"

3. The Parousia and the Savior

It is alarming to see such widespread and unflappable faith in the person of Donald Trump — that his return to power will demonstrate fulfillment of some divine promise, the anticipated restoration of a savior, and birth of a new era. Metaphorically and mythologically the former President is depicted and viewed by his followers as a prophet, redeemer, and avenger. The image is not unlike what we find in those words of St. John's Gospel.

> *I looked, and there before me was a white horse! Its rider held a bow, and he was given a crown, and he rode out as a conqueror bent on conquest.* (7)

This is what many Evangelicals seem to have been anticipating, and what the Christian Nationalists have been vociferously and violently promoting. They are signaling that the next Trump inauguration will bring a *parousia* or Second Coming of sorts — delivered and all wrapped up in biblical promises that were foretold. As well, Mr. Trump's ascension to the seat of power will be heralded as a call to arms and, as promised, a time of retribution.

There is a genuine experience of paranoia and distress creeping in and among the Christian faithful — those anxiously awaiting a return of their once and future king. It is also clearly the case that the apostle Paul was himself living in constant distress, anxiously anticipating the *End Time*. In fact, on the heels of his own conversion, Paul admits 'absolute distress' just waiting on the *parousia*, and working tirelessly to keep his churches focused on the coming event of Christ.(8)

Besides other things, I am under daily pressure because of my anxiety . . . (9)

Or again:

I came to you in weakness and in fear and in much trembling. . . (10)

In his analysis of St. Paul's personality, Heidegger also addresses the apostle's deep anxiety:

This distress articulates the authentic situation of Paul; it determines each moment of this life. He is constantly beset by suffering and anguish, despite his joy as apostle. (11)

His crucial role in spreading the Good News notwithstanding, Paul remained riddled with a self-effacing self-doubt as he himself testified to again and again:

On behalf of such a one I will boast, but on my own behalf I will not boast, except of my weaknesses... Therefore, to keep me from being too elated, a thorn was given me in the flesh, a messenger

of Satan to torment me, to keep me from
being too elated. (12)

And while Paul never once mentions the
actual timing of the *parousia*, he confirms
it will come unexpectedly and without
notice.

> *Now concerning the times and the*
> *seasons, brothers and sisters, you do*
> *not need to have anything written to*
> *you. For you yourselves know very well*
> *that the day of the Lord will come like a*
> *thief in the night.* (13)

4. "In Illo Tempore, Ab Origine" (14)

Myth-making stems from some of the
earliest stirrings of human creativity,
including the sacred stories found within
the Old and New Testaments. Throughout
prehistory and history, myths have served
to ground societies by anchoring
individuals to their community as well as
their surrounding environs. But given their
existential bearing, myths may also be
interpreted as relevant to a broad array of

current social or historical events — bestowing a unique status upon otherwise mundane states of affairs. And just as we may demythologize primal narrations, disclosing their underlying existential themes, so too can historical personages or events become mythologized, bestowed with a special, almost sacred status or legitimacy by means of the mythic narration.

In this light, we should understand that it is the mythologically-charged anticipation of the return of their savior Trump that motivates the Evangelicals along with their volatile brethren — the Christian Nationalists. And, it is precisely such faith that continues to drive a sharp wedge into the body politic of American society. This explains the odd case of Mr. Trump and his loyal following — turning the most ordinary of historical figures into a mythic hero for an inordinate plurality of Americans.

Furthermore, the mythic imagination has an almost limitless capacity to overwhelm present reality and create a life-world of its very own making. The subject of myth or the myth-maker may also be taken over by the persona of the mythic hero himself, living a mythical life to its bitter end. Mr. Trump and his entourage are consumed by the mythic reality that has been established. And they will now do whatever it takes to live out these mythological images, including rounding up nonbelievers, deporting the naysayers, or killing infidels, if required. Donald Trump himself has been consumed by his own mythological imagination. Because he was just a shallow, already empty shell of a person, he was able to put on this new 'shaman's cloak' (so to speak), and not just play the part but become the hero, now untethered and unconstrained by any convention or historical reality. As a myth-maker, Candidate Trump is the prime mover of this story, enabling his followers to partake in that special status accorded to a pristine time of the origins — '*in illo tempore, ab origine'* — anchoring the present moment within a meaning-filled and foundational framework already foretold in their Holy Book.

'Agnosis' and the Re-founding of America

1. Pilgrims and Priests

Right now you must be asking yourself: 'Okay, so what the hell does *agnosis* mean anyway?' Derived from Greek ἀγνωσία (*agnosia*) — meaning 'ignorance' or 'lack of knowledge' — *agnosis* is the opposite of the term *gnosis*. It is, as well, the root of our English word *agnostic* — referring to individuals who claim to have neither faith nor disbelief in the existence of God. And it is on this most menacing precipice that our current inquiry takes flight.

Reflecting upon our country's founding in the seventeenth century, we may recall that America — more than once described as a 'shining city upon a hill' — was first and foremost a refuge for those trying to flee religious persecution in their homeland. Freedom of religious belief was a principal reason for many, if not most, of the early settlers relocating to the New World. But today it feels increasingly as though America has become home only for those willing to testify to the divinity of Jesus — in short, for those adhering to one of the various denominations of Christianity. The non-Christian faithful, as well as non-believers more generally, are becoming increasingly marginalized — even labeled Un-American. And while the earliest colonies were forged from genuine struggles over religious freedom, the Puritans arriving from England displayed a fairly unforgiving intolerance for other expressions of faith, including the more primal beliefs of Native Americans already inhabiting the land.

Be that as it may, America was not founded as a refuge for any particular faith or set of religious convictions. In addition to the potential economic opportunities afforded settlers in the New World, this emerging country served equally well as refuge to those seeking to practice their faith without the fear of persecution they experienced in England. And, as the influx of immigrant pioneers expanded largely at the expense of the indigenous inhabitants, a governing body was soon established with ideals demanding respect and freedom for any and all persons regardless of their race, religious faith, or affiliation.

With boatloads of Huguenots, Catholics, Jews, Calvinists, Pietists, Presbyterians, Baptists, and Quakers then arriving in growing numbers on their shores, most colonists were forced to display some modicum of religious tolerance. Indeed, Pennsylvania's first constitution positively affirmed that all peoples who agreed to live peacefully would never be "molested or prejudiced for their religious persuasion."

But governance like this was, and remains, a delicate balance. Democracy dies when or where diversity of belief, opinion, or thought is in some way restricted, outlawed, or otherwise penalized. So what are the options for us now in the land of the free and home of the brave?

2. A Complicated History

By its very nature, then, religion is a rather sticky and complicated affair. Respect for religious difference is, more often than not, both a personal and a cultural struggle. We have witnessed this in spades most recently in the ongoing war between Israeli forces and Hamas fighters along the Gaza Strip — Israel responding to lethal attacks on their towns and settlements including the killing of innocent concertgoers in the Negev Desert. Of course, religious wars have been a source of carnage from the beginning of history, and most specifically within those countries comprising the area known as the

'Fertile Crescent' including the location of the ancient civilizations of Sumer, Akkad, and the Babylonian Empire. The Jewish people themselves were held captive in Babylon for over fifty years beginning approximately 586 BCE, before being allowed to return to their homeland in Jerusalem.

But religion and religious intolerance is a principal source of violence within our own day and country as well. It could be argued in fact that the most recent attacks (including that on the US Capital) were perpetrated by those adhering to extremely volatile philosophies both emboldening and emboldened by a variety of Christian Conservatives on the Right. It seems that we are in the midst of a spreading religious war precisely here in the homeland. This began even before the book-banning, book-burning, travel bans, family separation, outlawing of abortions, restricting asylum seekers, as well as other civil rights infringements. Not surprisingly, such legal and extra-legal efforts have culminated in various mob scenes including Neo-Nazi marches, street violence, as well as a full-scale attempt to overturn our civil and political order.

An extreme form of Christian Nationalism has been planted and is growing on American soil. The reactionary behaviors of such believers have been attended to and watered by a very specific strain of Right-leaning extremist religiosity. Of course, religious wars have haunted Europe and the Middle East for millennia. But now a full-scale religious battle threatens to engulf our own country. By and large, this conflict is a result of cultural differences in evidence as certain groups seek to dictate national norms and behaviors. Yet, by the numbers the American appetite for religion may itself be on the wane. Indeed, a recent poll suggests that nearly 25% of Americans identify as having no specific religious affiliation. That is as close to agnostic as one can get.

And lest we forget, that charlatan, Donald Trump, played the part of a born-again Christian in order to secure loyalty from his religiously-affiliated followers on the extreme Right of the political spectrum. In point of fact, this segment of the US population appears to be growing. Indeed, Christian Nationalism has become a rallying cry for more than one hundred congressional Republicans including the likes of Lauren Bobert, Mo Brooks, Madison Cawthorn, Matt Gaetz, Louie Gohmert, Paul Gosar, Marjorie Taylor Greene, Jim Jordan, Kevin McCarthy, Steve Scalise, and we mustn't forget, the scabrous Governor of Florida and Presidential candidate, Ron DeSantis. In fact, a significant number of Republicans actually argue that America is a Christian nation. And, unfortunately, we will see some of those running for public office with even more vociferous positions in the next set of elections.

3. Final Thoughts

The questions we must now ask do not have simple answers. But ask them, we must. For example, how is it possible to reverse such thinking in a world already gone astray? How do we overcome the parochial vision and shrill voices of those adhering to one faith without regard for those clinging to yet another? Have religious orthodoxies so corrupted our humanity and capacity for understanding that we can no longer be with and alongside one another? And what, in short, can be done to moderate this increasingly belligerent state of affairs? I suggest we begin somewhat gingerly, briefly exploring the concept of *agnosis*.

Instead of claiming certain knowledge of God, perhaps we should learn to enjoy, or at least appreciate, a respectful 'ignorance' or 'not knowing' — and leave the mysteries of the godhead to the *gnostics*. After all, nearly a quarter of Americans already identify as religiously unaffiliated.

So what would be wrong with installing an *agnostic* in the presidential suite at the White House and re-founding our beloved country on the softer saddle of *agnosis*. In short, what if we testify that the mysteries of divinity should be left to the priests, rabbis, ministers, mullahs and imams, as well as to their respective flocks, while allowing the disbelievers among us to meditate upon life as they see fit. After all, let us not forget what our founders wrote back in the day:

> *Congress shall make no law respecting an establishment of religion, or prohibiting the free exercise thereof.*

This clause in the First Amendment to our Constitution affirms in its very structure not only freedom of religious belief but freedom from religion as well. (Just ask Ron Reagan, Jr.) In fact, it could be argued that the phrase requires that members of Congress make NO decisions affecting all Americans based upon religious belief or affiliation. If they do so, that law would itself be establishing and imposing a religion upon the entire electorate, non-believers as well as the great diversity of believers. Religious doctrines need to be parked at the doors of Congress along with any and all firearms. This would include any prayers offered by the Congressional Chaplain (more than an oxymoron). Indeed, perhaps there should never have been a chaplain in Congress to begin with.

As our world shrinks, these are more than just the rantings of a madman; they are preliminary reflections on the predicament we find ourselves in both domestically and internationally. Yet, it is incumbent upon us to find ways of moving beyond the impasse of religious faith, particularly in the political arena, to try to understand one another from outside the prism of religious conviction.

Notes

(1) Andrew Torba, Andrew Isker, *Christian Nationalism*, Independent Pub., Sept., 2022.

(2) 1 Corinthians 1:4 & 7

(3) Acts 9:3

(4) 1 Corinthians 15: 8-10

(5) 1 Thessalonians 4:14

(6) Ed Kilgore, 'Do Evangelicals Think Trump Is Jesus?' *Intelligencer*, May 8, 2023.

(7) Revelations, 6:2

(8) Martin Heidegger, *The Phenomenon of the Religious Life*, Indiana U., 2010, pp. 67-69

(9) 2 Corinthians 11:28

(10) 1 Corinthians 2:4

(11) Heidegger, Ibid.

(12) 1 Corinthians 12: 5-7

(13) 1 Thessalonians 5:1-2

(14) 'In That Time, at the Beginning'

www.ingramcontent.com/pod-product-compliance
Lightning Source LLC
Chambersburg PA
CBHW060546030426
42337CB00021B/4447